WHAT DOES A CENTER DO?

Paul Challen

PowerKiDS
press™

New York

Published in 2017 by The Rosen Publishing Group, Inc.
29 East 21st Street, New York, NY 10010

Copyright © 2017 by The Rosen Publishing Group, Inc.

Developed and Produced for Rosen by BlueApple*Works* Inc.
Managing Editor for BlueApple*Works*: Melissa McClellan
Art Director: Tibor Choleva
Designer: Joshua Avramson
Photo Research: Jane Reid
Editor: Kelly Spence

Basketball is a fluid game; care was taken and every effort was made to portray players in
the identified positions to highlight the content being featured.

Photo Credits: Title page borders, page borders michelaubryphoto/Shutterstock; title page, 10, 16, 19, 20, 21, 29 Louis Horch/
Dreamstime.com; page backgrounds Eugene Sergeev/Shutterstock; TOC Aleksandar Grozdanovski/Shutterstock; p. 4 T.J. Choleva
/EKS/Shutterstock; p. 5 Pavel L Photo and Video/Shutterstock.com; p. 6, 15, 26 left Keith Allison/Creative Commons; p. 7, 9, 10, 11,
14, 17, 18, 22 Aspen Photo/Shutterstock.com; p. 7 top Donald Barnat/Creative Commons; p. 8 Ververidis Vasilis/Shutterstock.com;
p. 12 Richard Paul Kane/Shutterstock.com; p. 13 Aspenphoto/Dreamstime.com; p. 17 top, 19 top, 27 top Jerry Coli/Dreamstime.
com; p. 23 technotr/iStockphoto; p. 24 Matthew Jacques/Shutterstock; p. 25 Steve Debenport/iStockphoto; p. 26 right Natursports/
Dreamstime.com; p. 27 left Verse Photography/Creative Commons; p. 27 right Daniel Raustadt/Dreamstime.com; p. 28 Monkey
Business Images/Shutterstock

Cataloging-in-Publication Data
Names: Challen, Paul.
Title: What does a center do? / Paul Challen.
Description: New York : PowerKids Press, 2017. | Series: Basketball smarts | Includes index.
Identifiers: ISBN 9781508150497 (pbk.) | ISBN 9781508150442 (library bound) |
    ISBN 9781508150329 (6 pack)
Subjects: LCSH: Center play (Basketball)--Juvenile literature.
Classification: LCC GV887.74 C53 2017 | DDC 796.323'2--dc23

Manufactured in the United States of America
CPSIA Compliance Information: Batch #BS16PK For Further Information contact: Rosen Publishing, New York, New York at 1-800-237-9932

CONTENTS

THE BASKETBALL TEAM

Teamwork is everything in basketball. On the court, the team is made up of five positions: point guard, shooting guard, small forward, power forward, and center. Each player has a different job to do, both on **offense**, when their team has the ball, and on **defense**, when their opponents do. In practice, players work on individual skills like shooting, **dribbling**, and **passing**.

Each position is assigned a number. This diagram shows where each player is typically positioned when the team is trying to score.

*1. **Point guard:** The player who is responsible for leading the team and creating scoring opportunities.*

*2. **Shooting guard:** A player who focuses on scoring baskets, often from a **wing**, or side, position.*

*3. **Small forward:** A speedy, skilled player who can score baskets.*

*4. **Power forward:** A player who uses their size to play close to the basket to **rebound** and defend.*

*5. **Center:** Usually the tallest player on the team, the center plays near the net and shoots, rebounds, and blocks shots.*

All good basketball teams balance a strong offense and solid defense. They try to score baskets on offense, moving the ball as a team by dribbling and passing. On defense, teammates combine their efforts to stop the other team from scoring. Teams prepare for game day by running drills and plays that create game-like situations. It is important for a team to communicate and work together at practice and in games to play to the best of its ability.

The center (marked with a yellow arrow throughout this book) usually plays close to the basket, also known as the "low **post**." On defense this allows them to protect the basket, and on offense it places them in a good position to score.

CENTERING THE TEAM

The center on a basketball team combines with the small forward and power forward to make up a team's **frontcourt**. The player in this position is almost always the tallest on the team, and uses their size and skill to lead the squad on offense and defense under the basket. Centers must be good at scoring baskets from close range, and at blocking shots in their defensive end.

The center is often the tallest player on the team. Joakim Noah (left) stands 6 feet 11 inches (2.11 m) tall. JaVale McGee (right) is 7 feet (2.13 m) tall. Both players are about the average height for a center.

The tallest athletes to ever play in the NBA were both centers. Romanian Gheorghe Mureşan and Manute Bol of Sudan both stood at 7 feet 7 inches (2.3 m) tall, and used their height to score points and block shots. At 7 feet 2 inches (2.2 m), Margo Dydek (right) was the tallest player to ever play in the WNBA.

On offense and defense, the center is often a team's closest player to the basket. This area is called the "low post." On offense, it is against the rules for players to stay in the **key** for longer than three seconds. If they do, the **referee** will blow the whistle and call a technical **foul**. Centers move continuously in and out of low-post positions, moving with their opponents and battling for position.

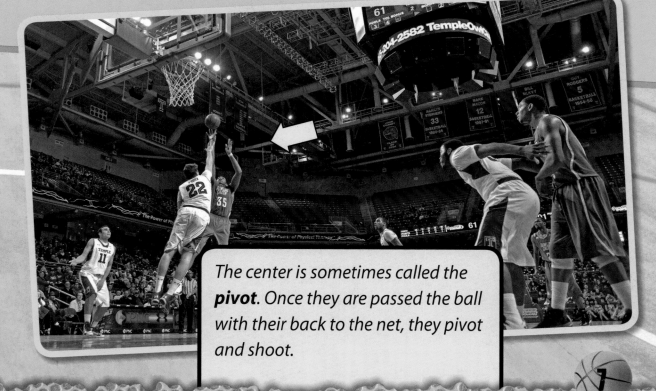

The center is sometimes called the **pivot**. Once they are passed the ball with their back to the net, they pivot and shoot.

OFFENSIVE STRATEGY

Coaches who want to focus on their center's skill will use a half-court offense. In this attack, a team passes the ball among teammates in the opponents' half of the court, trying to get the ball to their "big men," the power forward and center, for high-percentage shots close to the basket. A team looking to run a half-court offense has to be patient. It can take a while to work the ball around with passing and dribbling, especially against a tough defense.

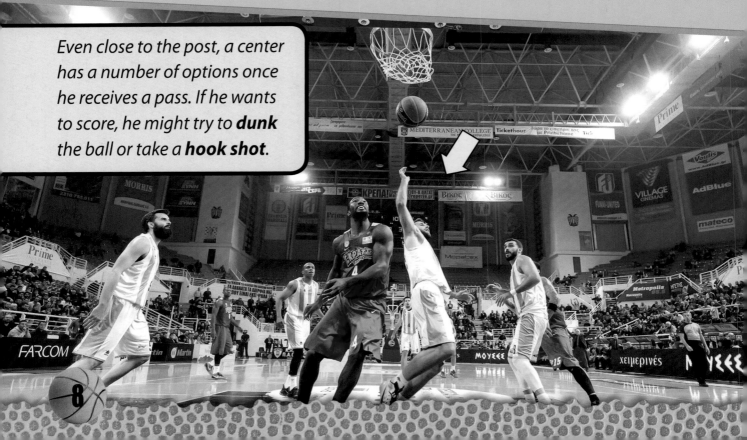

Even close to the post, a center has a number of options once he receives a pass. If he wants to score, he might try to **dunk** the ball or take a **hook shot**.

Because of their size and skills, some centers are the focus of a team's offense. The coach will design special plays to maximize this player's contributions. Statistically, centers often have a very high shooting percentage compared to their teammates because their up-close shots have a better chance of going in than shots taken from farther out.

Centers tend to take a large number of shots. The closer you are to the basket, the more likely your shot is to go in. Being able to quickly get into a good scoring position after receiving the ball is an important skill for centers.

DEFENSIVE STRATEGY

The center is crucial to any team's defense. Many centers are very quick for their size. They need to know how to use their strength and agility to "protect the paint" close to the basket. If a teammate is beaten to the basket, the center will often shift out of position to stop a shooter with a **blocked shot**. On defense, centers must combine their physical skills with the ability to read offensive attacks coming down the court.

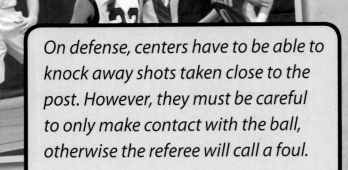

On defense, centers have to be able to knock away shots taken close to the post. However, they must be careful to only make contact with the ball, otherwise the referee will call a foul.

On many teams, the center is the hardest-working player on defense because of all of the responsibilities they have for protecting the basket. Although basketball does not have as much contact as football or hockey, centers still face a lot of pushing and bumping when they defend, usually against the opposing team's center. Players in this position must have strong legs and arms to handle this physical play.

Action close to the post can get very physical. A center has to be able to stand their ground. The position requires both upper and lower body strength to keep from getting pushed around.

JUMP BALL

At the start of a game, and to restart the game or begin a new period, the jump ball occurs. It takes place either at the center-court circle, or at one of the circles at the top of each key. Each team picks a player to take the jump ball, and the referee stands between them. The ref tosses the ball high in the air, and the two players leap up and try to tip the ball to a teammate.

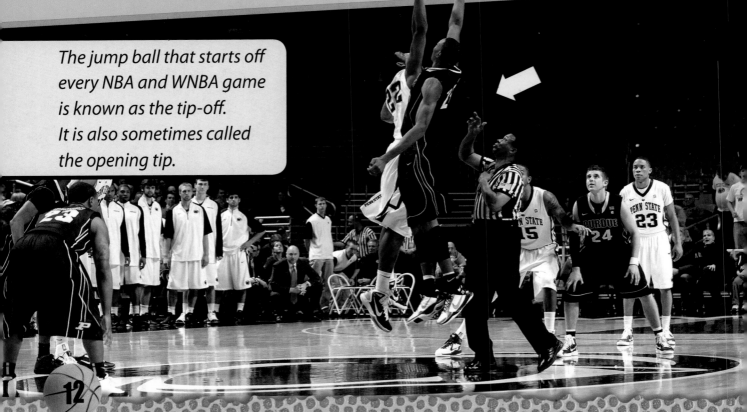

The jump ball that starts off every NBA and WNBA game is known as the tip-off. It is also sometimes called the opening tip.

The center usually lines up for the jump ball. As the team's tallest player, the center usually has the best chance of winning the ball. Being able to leap high from a standing start is crucial, but timing and the ability to judge the direction of the ball out of the referee's hand is also important.

The start of the game isn't the only time a jump ball occurs. When two opponents each have their hands on the ball, and one is unable to get it away from the other, the ref will blow the whistle and call a jump ball.

SHOT BLOCKING

On the defensive side of the game, blocking shots is one of a center's most important jobs. Centers often lead their teams in shots blocked. Even if they are not actually able to swat their opponents' shots away every time, the threat of a block means that offensive players will avoid shooting from close range. Instead, they might try to make more difficult shots from outside the key.

*Stopping **layups** is one of a center's main responsibilities. Not only does it lower the offensive player's shooting percentage, also the fewer shots the opposing team sinks, the more likely the other team is to win!*

*It is against the rules of basketball to **goaltend**, or touch a ball that is inside what is known as the "cylinder"— an imaginary circle above the rim of the basket. Because any shot inside this area has a chance of going in, it is illegal to interfere with it. If a defensive player goaltends, the basket is counted. If an offensive player goaltends, possession switches to the other team and any basket that was made does not count.*

It is important for a center to try to avoid fouling a shooter when going for a block, as this will lead to the shooter being awarded **free throws** by the referee. Most good shot blockers learn to knock shots away with their blocking hand straight up in the air. A center also must be able to direct the blocked shot to another defensive teammate, or try to gain possession of the ball themselves.

This center is going all out to block the basket from going in. It is important for the center to time their jump to knock the ball away.

GRAB THAT BALL

On offense, centers not only help their team by scoring, but also by "crashing the boards" and winning as many offensive rebounds as they can. Controlling rebounds off of their teammates' missed shots can lead to extra shots and extra chances to score. These are known as second chance points and can make the difference between a win and a loss in a close game.

Players often miss on their first attempt at a shot. If a center can win an offensive rebound, it gives their team another chance to score.

Wilt Chamberlain holds the NBA record for most rebounds per game average. He played in the league from 1959 to 1973. Throughout his career, Chamberlain averaged 22.9 rebounds a game. He was followed closely by his rival, Bill Russell of the Boston Celtics, who averaged 22.5 rebounds per game.

Defensive rebounds are also important to a team's success. If the center can limit the opposing team to one shot per possession, grab the rebound, and pass to a teammate, it reduces the number of scoring opportunities for the rival team. Limiting the number of shots an opponent can take is a great strategy for winning games.

After capturing a defensive rebound, a center will protect the ball while looking to pass or dribble the ball up the court.

BOXING OUT

Boxing out is a technique used by centers on both offense and defense. To box out an opponent, the center must stay between the player and the basket, battling for position to win the rebound. When boxing out for the rebound, it is important for the center to be strong and physical, but also smart and quick. They have to be aware of where the rebound will come down, as well as where their opponent is on the court.

Boxing out is an extremely physical maneuver. The center gets right up against the player he's guarding, faces the basket, and tries to physically back the opposing player up. They spread their arms wide to block off as large an area as possible for the opposing player to get around.

The center may also be called on to help execute the back screen play. This involves two teammates, neither of whom is in possession of the ball. The screening player takes up a position on the court and stands still. The other player, the "cutter," moves into position to receive a pass and runs closely by the screener. The player who was guarding the cutter runs into the screener, allowing the cutter to break free of their defender.

During the back screen play, the screener must stand still. If the screener moves while in contact with the player he or she is screening, the referee will call a foul.

GETTING THE PASS

As they get into position close to the basket, centers have to be ready at all times to receive a pass. This can come directly through the air, or in the form of a bounce pass off the court. Centers need good, "soft" hands to catch and control the ball. Once they have possession of the ball, they can quickly decide what to do as their next move.

Once a center receives a pass they need to quickly decide on the best course of action. Should they shoot immediately? Pass the ball? Or try to reposition themselves for an easier shot?

When the center receives the ball close to the basket in the post position, a second defender will often come to quickly double-team the center. Good centers can quickly recognize when they are being double-teamed, and pass the ball out of trouble to an open teammate who has been left unguarded.

A smart center can draw the attention of multiple defenders. Once he's covered, he can easily pass the ball to a teammate who is completely open.

SHOOTING THE BALL

Shooting the basketball requires strength and balance. Players also take some shots while on the move, so speed can be an advantage for a shooter as well. As a key part of a team's offense, centers are usually called on to be strong shooters and good scorers. Like all smart players, centers need to know what shots they can make consistently, and when it's a better option to pass the ball to an open teammate.

A good hook shot is a useful skill for a center to have. It is a one-handed shot in which a player arcs the ball over his head and into the basket. The player keeps the defender away by positioning their body in between their shooting hand and the defender.

As one of the biggest players on the court, centers also score a fair share of points by slamming the ball through the hoop from close range. These dunks can be made as solo moves, or on a high pass from a teammate that the center can catch and slam in. This impressive move is called an alley-oop. As well, since centers get fouled often, they usually get many chances to attempt free throws. Although this is a great chance to score points, many of the best centers have struggled at sinking free throws.

The slam dunk is one of the most exciting moves in the game. The player with the ball will leap off the floor and slam the ball right through the basket. This can be done with either one or two hands.

THE ROLE OF A COACH

Many basketball experts say that it is impossible to find a good team without also finding a good coach behind it. Coaches play a huge role in teaching players the skills they need to succeed on offense and defense. A coach also develops strategies and plays so that their team is able to score points and stop opponents.

Coaches can call a time-out to go over a play, or even give players a rest to slow down the game

As well as giving advice on the court, coaches also have an important role to play off the court. A healthy diet, rest, and recovery are all important parts of the game. For school teams, coaches also stress the importance of doing well in the classroom. Because of their important role in any team's offense or defense, centers can benefit a lot from a good coach.

Coaches don't just help their players develop their physical skills. They also help them develop a strong mental game. After all, a player who can shoot accurately, but falls apart the moment things get hard, isn't very useful to a team. Confidence, character, and sportsmanship are all important skills taught by a good coach.

THE BEST CENTERS

There have been hundreds of great centers, and basketball fans love to debate about who the best all-time players in this position have been. Bill Russell introduced a new style of defensive play and revolutionized the position playing for the Boston Celtics from 1956–1969. Other early greats were Wilt Chamberlain, Patrick Ewing, and Shaquille "Shaq" O'Neal.

Andre Drummond (left) is a young center who has played for the Detroit Pistons since he was drafted in 2012. His first year he was named to the NBA All-Rookie Second Team, and in 2016 he became an All-Star for the first time!

Center DeMarcus Cousins of the Sacramento Kings is one of the greatest young talents in the NBA. In 2010–11 he made the all-rookie team in his first season, and in 2015 was an NBA All-Star.

DID YOU KNOW?

Many fans believe that Kareem Abdul-Jabbar was the greatest NBA center in history. He led the Los Angeles Lakers to six NBA titles, and was named the league's MVP six times as well. At 7 feet 2 inches (2.2 m) tall, Kareem had an unstoppable hook shot that became known as the "sky hook."

Marc Gasol (left), who grew up in Spain, plays for the Memphis Grizzlies. Gasol is known as a strong defensive center. He has played in two NBA All-Star games and also won an Olympic silver in 2008 and 2012 playing for Team Spain.

In the WNBA, Britney Griner (right) of the Phoenix Mercury led her team to the 2014 title, has made three All-Star games, and has won the Defensive Player of the Year award twice.

BE A GOOD SPORT

Basketball demands drive and determination, and games can be intense. But remembering to show respect for your opponents, teammates, referees, and fans is very important. Good sportsmanship means keeping your cool on the court. Coaches, parents, and players can also do a lot to make sure everyone has fun by keeping the game fair, clean, and honest.

It's important for all team members to be a good sport both on and off the court. From the sidelines and on the court, players should always cheer on and support their teammates.

Because the center is so often in the middle of the action during a game, this player can set an example for teammates by playing hard but fair. Also, because so many offensive and defensive plays revolve around the center, players in this position can show leadership in practice sessions, demonstrating fair play and sportsmanship at all times. At the end of the game, make sure you give a firm handshake to the officials, as well as a high five to players on the other team. Praise your own team's efforts as well.

With such a central role in a team's offense and defense, the center is often a role model for other players. A good center knows that following the rules and playing hard but fair is one of the most important parts of the game.

GLOSSARY

blocked shot Any offensive shot that is stopped, or "blocked," in mid-flight, on the way up, by a defensive player.

defense When a team tries to stop the team with the ball from scoring.

dribbling Moving the ball up the court by bouncing it with one hand at a time.

dunk A close-range shot executed by jumping up and slamming the ball through the hoop.

foul Committing an infraction of the rules of basketball, as determined by the referee in an official game.

free throws Uncontested shots taken from the free throw line that have been awarded after a foul.

frontcourt Where the center, small forward, and power forward play.

goaltend In basketball, when a player interferes with a shot above the rim of the basket.

hook shot An offensive shot taken by releasing the ball with one hand high overhead while the shooter's body is placed between the defender and the shooting hand.

key The area of a basketball court that is closest to the basket and marked off by a rectangle with a jump-ball circle at its top.

layups Moving basketball shots, taken by a player who dribbles, takes two quick steps while carrying the ball, and then shoots.

offense The part of basketball involving possession of the ball and attempts to score.

passing Throwing the ball through the air to a teammate.

pivot The point on which something turns.

post The area on a basketball court located between the basket and the free-throw line.

rebound To catch the ball after it bounces off the rim or backboard.

referee The person who enforces the on-court rules of a basketball game.

wing In basketball, one of the two sides of the court.

FOR MORE INFORMATION

FURTHER READING

Doeden, Matt. *Basketball Legends in the Making.* Mankato, MN: Capstone, 2014.

Donnelly, Patrick. *The Best NBA Centers.* Edina, MN: ABDO, 2015.

Editors of Sports Illustrated Kids, The. *Sports Illustrated Kids Big Book of Who: Basketball.* New York: Sports Illustrated, 2015.

Greve, Tom. *Basketball Centers.* Chicago: Britannica Digital Learning, 2013.

WEBSITES

Due to the changing nature of Internet links, PowerKids Press has developed an online list of websites related to the subject of this book. This site is updated regularly. Please use this link to access the list:

www.powerkidslinks.com/bs/center

INDEX